A DEEP, ABIDING LOVE

A Deep, Abiding LOVE

Pondering Life's Depth with Julian of Norwich

JENNIFER LYNN CHRIST

TWENTY-THIRD PUBLICATIONS
One Montauk Avenue, Suite 200
New London, CT 06320
(860) 437-3012 or (800) 321-0411
www.twentythirdpublications.com

ISBN: 978-1-62785-315-6
Library of Congress Control Number: 2017944489
Printed in the U.S.A.

Contents

Journaling with Julian

I have found this statement of Father John-Julian, OJN, to be very true for me: "Julian stands forward as a primary voice of clarity and hope."

I begin this book in late mid-life, persevering in a forty-four-year marriage that is mostly wonderful but has endured some painful, very fragile times. I am currently "mothering from the sidelines" four adult children, some of whom are currently experiencing "the slings and arrows of outrageous fortune" in their adult lives from which I cannot save them. I have found I cannot pray away their life lessons. I also am Grandma to four precious small boys and one baby girl who bring indescribable joy into the everyday, just by their contagious grins and insatiable eagerness for life.

I first met Julian on a private retreat. Perusing the gift shop of the monastery, I came across a daybook of short quotes and prayers, the title assuring that *all shall be well*. I bought it, was comforted and intrigued by it, prayed it for one month, and then promptly forgot about it. Some two years later I was doing research at the Saint Francis de Sales Seminary library, and near to the books pertinent to my research was a section of books about Julian of Norwich. I pulled out the book I was seeking for my work, but it was too tightly shelved, causing Julian to come rushing out at me, hitting me on the head as her *A Revelation of Divine Love* fell to the floor. As I picked it up I realized this was the same mystic who had kept me company for thirty days two years ago. I opened the book, began to read, and was flooded with tears of consolation. Our family had been experiencing an anguishing period of upset and confusion with our adolescent second son. My heart was wrenched, my mind worried, and my psyche worn from the current trials as our beloved son tore away from our family in a most painful manner. We were in the midst of a harrowing time, the likes of which our family had never before experienced. Julian said again and again that *all shall be well.*

Over the last several years I have given talks and preached retreats on Julian's consoling message. I have drawn parallels between her times and ours: the many wars, scandals in the church, corruption in government, devastating waves of plague, disillusionment, and despair. I have found Julian's message of hope and joy in God's never-ending love for us to be a balm for our worldly troubles. I have been privileged and continue to be grateful to introduce others to this blessed mystic who first startled me and then opened my heart with her clear, hopeful message.

Julian lived in fourteenth-century England, in the bustling mercantile town of Norwich. She was born in 1342 or 1343 and lived until at least 1416. We know precious little about her life, but what we do know is wonderfully significant. At age thirty and a half (as she relates), on what she believed to be her deathbed, Julian received sixteen "shewings" (Middle English) or "showings" in which God revealed his great love for humankind. She survived her illness and quickly wrote down what she had seen, heard, and come to understand in these encounters. Julian then became an anchoress, living enclosed in a small dwelling called an anchorhold, which was attached to the church of St. Julian in Norwich. The next forty years of her life were spent there praying, sewing clothes for the poor, receiving visitors, and acting as a spiritual director for the town. We know she also spent more time and reflection on those original visions and came to write an expanded version of them called *A Revelation of Divine Love.*

Julian came to know God as *Maker*, *Lover*, and *Keeper*. In her writings we come to know the God she saw who loves us unconditionally, uses even our sinfulness to a good end, and will never abandon his creation, making *all things well.* Julian knew pain, and knew with great certainty that suffering is interwoven with the human journey. But she was shown and shares with us a way through the pain, a larger view of a God who uses everything we suffer toward the ultimate reality of his divine will worked out in creation. Julian, in her quiet, unassuming earnestness shares the gift of her visions, offering us hope and joy in the midst of our divine/human life circumstances.

Perhaps you, dear reader, in *your* everyday life circumstances, in *your* present state of heart, need to hear of God's deep, abiding love for *you*, and that *all shall be well* in God's greater plan for *your* life. Scholars have called Julian a *theological optimist*. Just as in my first encounter with her, her words gently encourage me and inspire me every time I go to her for prayer and reflection. I offer you a simple introduction to Julian and an opportunity to be with her while pondering some deep questions about your life in a journal. I invite you to spend some time in her little cell, sitting with her, stroking her cat, and being both challenged and consoled by her message.

He Is Our Clothing

I saw that He is to us everything that is good
and comfortable for us.
He is our clothing which for love
enwraps us,
holds us,
and all encloses us
because of His tender love,
so that He may never leave us.

I have a favorite afghan my husband gave me as a gift. It is Wedgewood blue with a pattern of dogwood blossoms and branches, said in some old legends to be the wood of the cross. This afghan has companioned me for many years now. It went with me to my first yoga classes before I purchased a proper mat. It served as my meditation "cushion" for years. When I had an exhausting sixty-hour-per-week position in a parish, with four growing children and a husband at home, it helped me to make the transition from demanding, people-intensive work, to demanding, people-intensive home. I asked my family for fifteen undisturbed minutes when I came home. I went in my room, shut the door, and crawled head first under my afghan, totally enfolding myself in its familiar comfort. A permanent fixture on my couch, my afghan snuggles me on chilly evenings during "book time." Julian tells us that at *all times* we are held tenderly in God's love. Why do I so often forget this?

Under what conditions do you feel held? When do you experience a sense of comfort and safety? When do you feel most loved?

God is enwrapping, holding,
and enclosing me in tender love.

MANTRA FOR MEDITATION

The Hazelnut

He showed a little thing,
the size of a hazelnut
in the palm of my hand,
and it was as round as a ball.
I looked at it with the eye of my understanding and thought:
"what can this be?"

And it was generally answered thus:
"It is all that is made."

Have you done some traveling in your life? Have you flown in a plane over the vast ocean, over mountains that appeared below as toy forms for a model railroad setup? Have you hiked a long, long way and known distance in your whole body, not merely your feet? Have you had some experience of the vastness of our planet? This little planet, one among many other planets and stars in this one galaxy, one among many, many galaxies? The small hazelnut Julian saw in her hand, a mere bit, she was told, is all of creation. I tremble then to try to fathom how big is God! I won't try; it is beyond me to comprehend, and yet it is truth as Julian tells it.

A term of measurement used in cooking in Julian's time, **"the size of a hazelnut"** was used by her to stress the littleness of creation when compared to the utter vastness of the Creator.

Take a moment to ponder the awesomeness of God by observing both the vastness of creation (the big blue sky) and the intricate littleness of creation (an insect dutifully going about its work). God the Creator of all has also created you in your human complexity. What would be an appropriate expression of your gratitude?

The Maker, Lover, and Keeper

In this little thing [the hazelnut] I saw three characteristics:
the first is that God made it,
the second is that God loves it,
the third, that God keeps it.

But what did I observe in that?

Truly the Maker, the Lover, and the Keeper for,
until I am in essence one-ed to Him,
I can never have full rest nor true joy
(that is to say, until I am made so fast to Him
that there is absolutely nothing that is created
separating my God and myself).

As Julian tells it, God is our Maker, our Lover, and our Keeper. He is all this without my even thinking about it. This is why I exist, why I don't disintegrate into mere nothingness. All I am, all I think, all I do in my life is because God sustains my being and allows it life and function. I experience this *oneness* when I love, when I am loved, and when my life is undeservedly flooded with grace. But it is true even when I don't know that it is. I am *one-ed* to God, even on days of desolation, confusion, and restlessness. I am *one-ed* to God even in my grief, my challenges, and my pain. During these times I think I am alone, but God is closer than ever. Like the iron-on patches my Mom used to mend the holes in my jeans, God and I are fused together.

When do you feel closest to God? When does God seem very far away? Why do you think God allows us to have both of these experiences? In what ways can you draw nearer to God in your everyday awareness?

For I am convinced that neither death, nor life, nor angels, nor principalities, nor present things, nor future things, nor powers, nor height, nor depth, nor any other creature will be able to separate us from the love of God in Christ Jesus our Lord. ROMANS 8:38–39

The Yearning Soul

Also our Lord God showed
that it is full pleasure to Him
that a pitiable soul come to Him
nakedly and plainly and simply.
For this is the natural yearning of the soul,
thanks to the touching of the Holy Spirit,
according to the understanding that I have in
this showing—
"God, of Thy goodness, give me Thyself"
for Thou art enough to me,...

and He has made us only for Himself
and restored us by His blessed passion
and ever keeps us in His blessed love.

Sometimes I feel such desolation that I doubt God's existence. This comes after I have prayed and prayed and no answer comes. The heavens seem locked and vacated. Is God really there or is my faith something I made up just to get me through the toughest days? In these times I am truly a "pitiable soul." Problems and complexities of problems mount up and there is nowhere to go for solace. Then, gradually, "the natural yearning of the soul" like a homing pigeon seeking home, turns to the Lover, the Maker, the Keeper. I can choose to resist this natural movement, but not really for very long. A tiny magnet deep within me is powerfully attracted to a much, much larger magnet. I am helpless and must turn. When I do, I suddenly know I am in right relationship, and know that it would be impossible to find consolation in any other place or person or human experience or material thing. Only God can ease the turmoil of the naked soul.

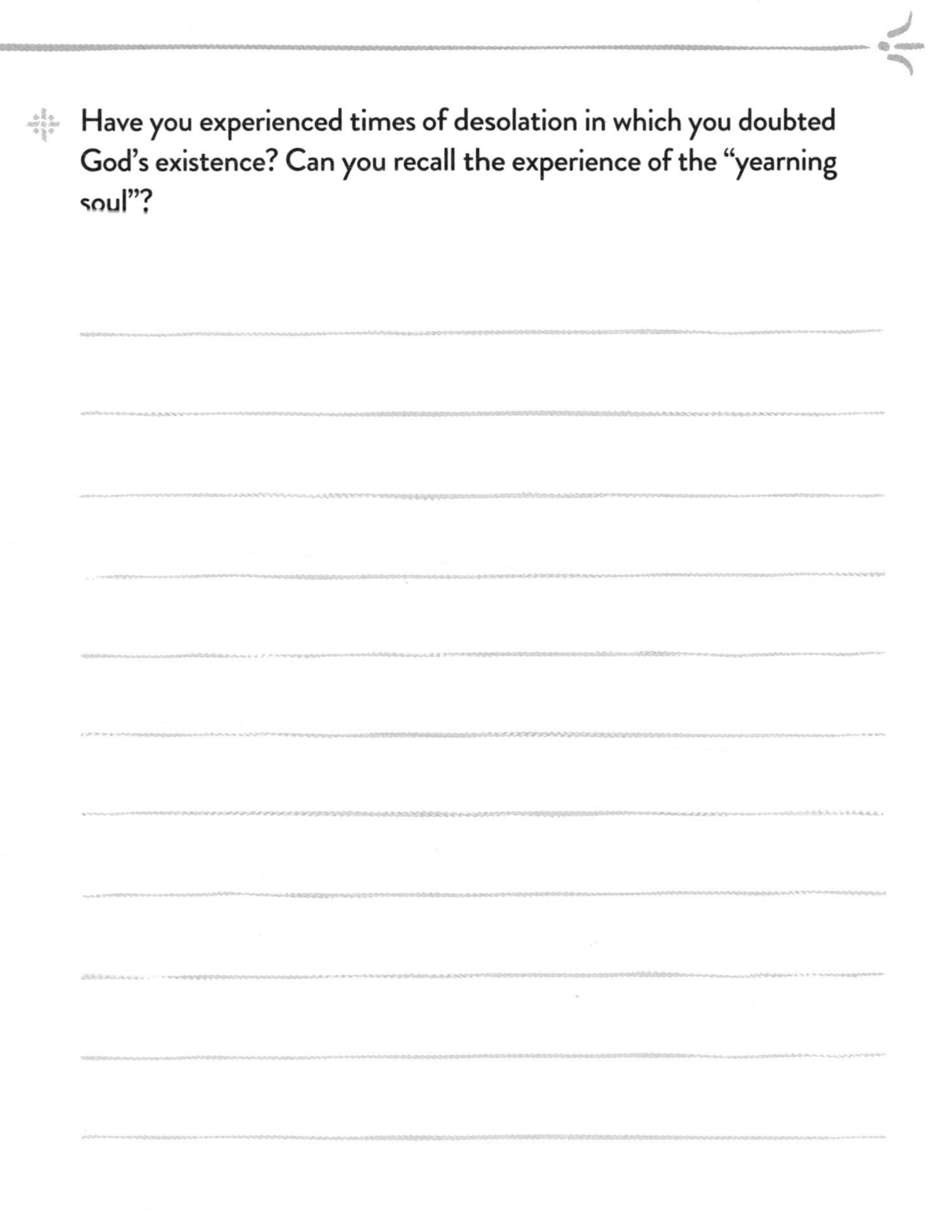

Have you experienced times of desolation in which you doubted God's existence? Can you recall the experience of the "yearning soul"?

Our hearts are restless until they rest in thee.

ST. AUGUSTINE

All the Blessed Company

We pray to Him by His sweet Mother's love
who bore Him,
but all the help we have from her is of His goodness.
And we pray by His Holy Cross that He died on,
but all the strength and the help that we have from
the cross is from His goodness.
And in the same way, all the help that we have from
special saints and all the blessed company of heaven
the dearworthy love and endless friendship
that we have from them—
it is from His goodness.

Most every day I pray the Rosary, usually while walking in the evening with my husband. I am tired and full of the troubles of the day. Out come the familiar, gently clicking beads. Mary is always there, taking my hand, saying, "Come walk with me and we'll sort it out." And by the time we have done our laps around the neighborhood and passed five statues of our Blessed Mother in people's gardens, she has led us back to the goodness of her Son's love. So too the saints. There is a heavenly friend for every problem I encounter. St. Anthony finds my lost earring, St. Monica understands my motherly worries, St. Francis greets me in my garden, St. Jude is in charge of those very tragic cases that come over the prayer network, and St. Joseph keeps us steady in our work and in our family. They all lead us back to Jesus and his goodness.

Who are the "intermediaries" in heaven to whom you turn? Do they help you to find the path back to our Lord? In what ways are their lives "signposts" for you on your divine/human journey?

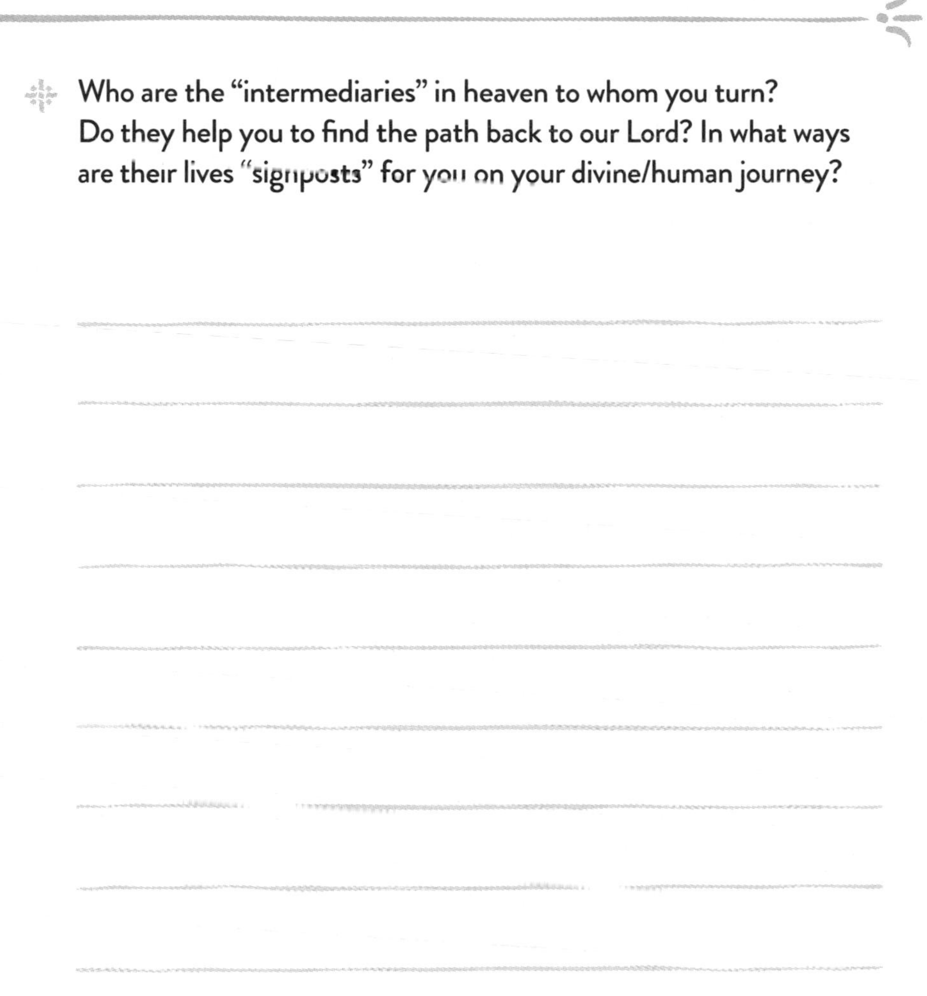

The wonderful thing about saints is that they were human. They lost their tempers, scolded God, were egotistical or testy or impatient in their turns, made mistakes and regretted them. Still they went on doggedly blundering toward heaven.

PHYLISS MCGINLEY

Cleave to Him

For as the body is clad in the clothes,
and the flesh in the skin,
and the bones in the flesh,
and the heart in the breast,
so are we, soul and body, clad in the goodness of God
and enclosed—yea, and even more intimately,
because all these others may waste
and wear away,
but the goodness of God is ever whole,
and nearer to us without any comparison.
For truly our Lover desires that our soul cleave to Him
with all its might and that we evermore
cleave to His goodness,
for of all things that heart can think,
this pleases God most and soonest succeeds.

Julian says that God desires our soul to *cleave* to him. Sometimes in my deepest times of trouble when all is tangled up in ego stupefaction, I can't see a way out. I can't see my way clear to peace again. I am caught in human messes! I cry out "Help!" or "Jesus, Mary, and Joseph have mercy on us!" or simply "Jesus!" I call these prayers my *clinging* prayers. Perhaps this is what Julian is speaking of in her use of the word *cleave*. God's goodness encloses us. How, in that enclosure, can we feel so alone and without succor? It seems that what is required is an act of will on our part to cry out, to cleave. Henri Nouwen says we must "hum in the darkness." I often light a candle, place it on my stovetop, and leave it burning throughout the day, reminding me that Christ is present, right here in the midst of my tangles. Sometimes I light several candles all at once against the darkness.

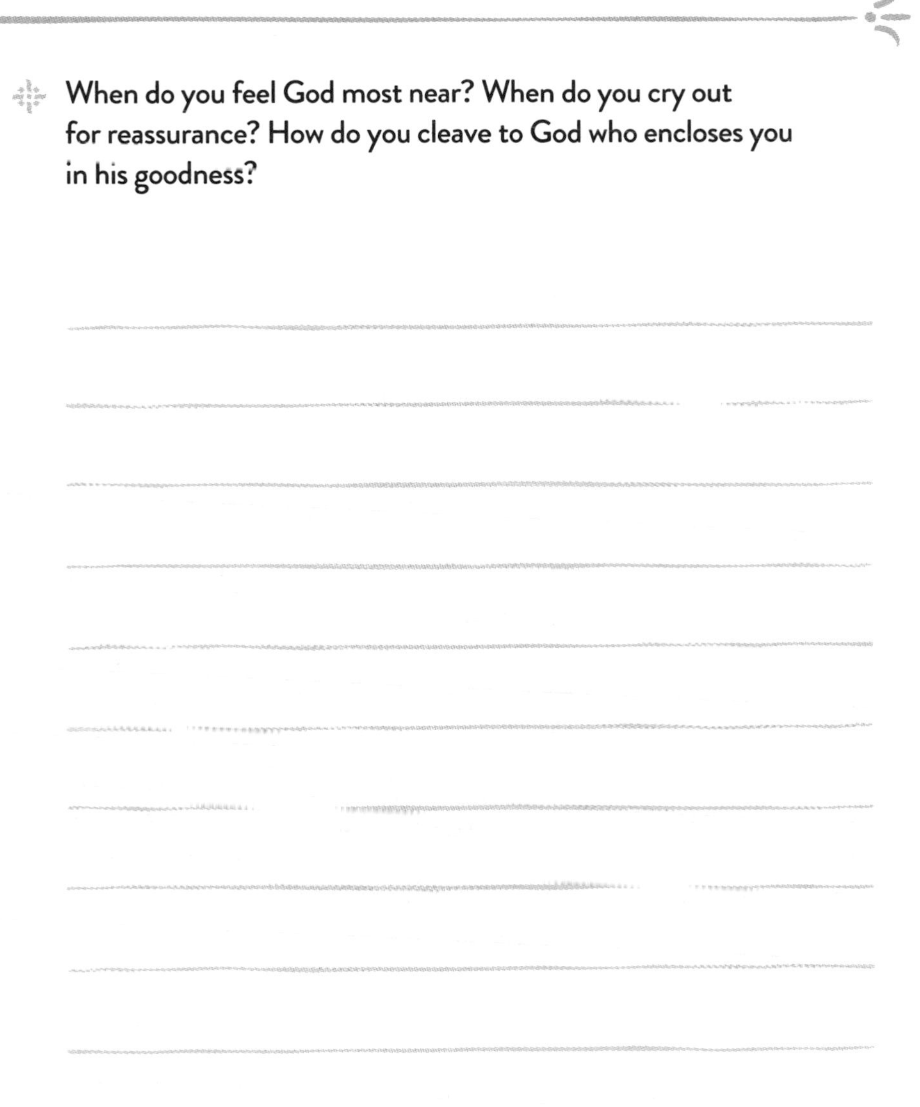

When do you feel God most near? When do you cry out for reassurance? How do you cleave to God who encloses you in his goodness?

Incline your ear, O Lord; answer me, for I am afflicted and poor. Keep my life, for I am devoted to you; save your servant who trusts in you.

PSALM 86:1–2

The Most Joy

Thus it fares between our Lord Jesus and ourselves;
for truly it is the most joy that can be, as I see it,
that He who is highest and mightiest,
noblest and worthiest,
is also lowliest and meekest,
most friendly and most gracious.

Julian speaks here of God's transcendence, his vastness and "otherness," and his immanence, his being here right now, involved in every little aspect of my life—simultaneously. This is such a mystery, I don't even tax my brain to try to figure it out. Yet I know it's true. I can ask God to help find me a parking spot; I beg God to help my grown kids figure out their lives. Same God: little requests and huge ones. Actually, the most friendly and most gracious immanent God is the one I get along with best. If he denies some of my little, daily requests, I can roll with that pretty well. It's the big life and death issues, the joys (not mere happiness in the moment) and sorrows, that keep me awake in the middle of the night. I long for Hannah's right leg to be healed, for her to figure out her life, for her to become financially secure and to use her many gifts for good. I beg for Andrew, who has such a loving heart, to at last find his soulmate. I ache that we humans are throwing sticks and stones and deadly bombs at each other. My heart mourns for some of my directees who suffer so in their tangled relationships. I can't reconcile a three-year-old with a brain tumor. I yearn for true joy, peace, and love that transcends ego. Like Saul Bellow's character in *Henderson the Rain King*, "I want, I want, I want." Yet these requests seem to take eternally forever, if ever. The great, big, highest, and mightiest God, who has a grand purpose in all these heartrending difficulties, is the hardest God for me to know.

What do you make of God's transcendence and God's immanence? Which God do you know best and how do you experience his friendliness and graciousness in your everyday life?

Not in This Lifetime, Not Yet

[And] This wishes Our Lord:
that we believe and trust,
enjoy and delight,
comfort and solace ourselves, as best we can.
with His grace and with His help,
until the time that we see His joy truly....

But no man can be aware of this marvelous friendliness
in this life,
unless he receives it by special showing from Our Lord,
or from a great abundance of grace inwardly given
from the Holy Spirit.

But faith and belief with love are worthy to have the reward,
and so it is received by grace—
for in faith with hope and love, our life is grounded.

Julian was given a great gift in her sixteen showings! She was shown *in fullness* the love God has for us and the joy that will be ours for all eternity. She was so anxious that we would see what she saw that she spent years in her anchorhold pondering what she was shown and trying to capture it in words so we would know it too. Most of us get only grace-filled glimpses that something truly joyful is ultimately in store for all of us. Last evening as my husband and I took our Rosary walk, the pinky blue evening sky, studded with whipped egg white clouds, beckoned us to another place, beyond our neighborhood of barking dogs and discordant leaf blowers. The place of peace, rest, and solace seemed so near, hanging just above the quotidian landscape, yet it also seemed eternally far off. Julian gives

us clear direction: believe, trust, enjoy, and delight; find comfort and solace; love, and hope *as best you can*, until you too are made aware of this *marvelous friendliness*. I'll try to do that today, as best I can.

Do you live your life in trust and hope? How do you find joy, delight, and comfort even now in this "already, but not yet" world?

Seeking Him

For I saw Him and still sought Him,
for we are now so blind and so unwise that we never
seek God until He of His goodness shows Himself to us;
and when we see anything of Him by grace, then
are we moved by the same grace to try with great
desire to see Him more perfectly.

And thus I saw Him and I sought Him,
and I possessed Him and I lacked Him.
And this is, and should be, our ordinary behavior in this life,
as I see it.

Julian describes a divine/human game of hide and seek. She found God. She desired to see him more perfectly, and then she lost him again. God's grace rules the game. We see God if he desires that we do. I notice we don't have a lot of control here; we only consent to play the game. Julian sees a proper order in this. In my lack of humility, I would like to have more say as to the rules, and I would like the game to go exactly by those rules—*my* rules. Ha! Fat chance of that, Julian tells us. So I must accept the rules of God's game of hide and seek. This is my struggle every day—to accept the divine plan. God is in control; I am not. It is in those moments of surrender that he so often shows himself unexpectedly, like a heaven-scented, orange-tinged, yellow rose blooming in November.

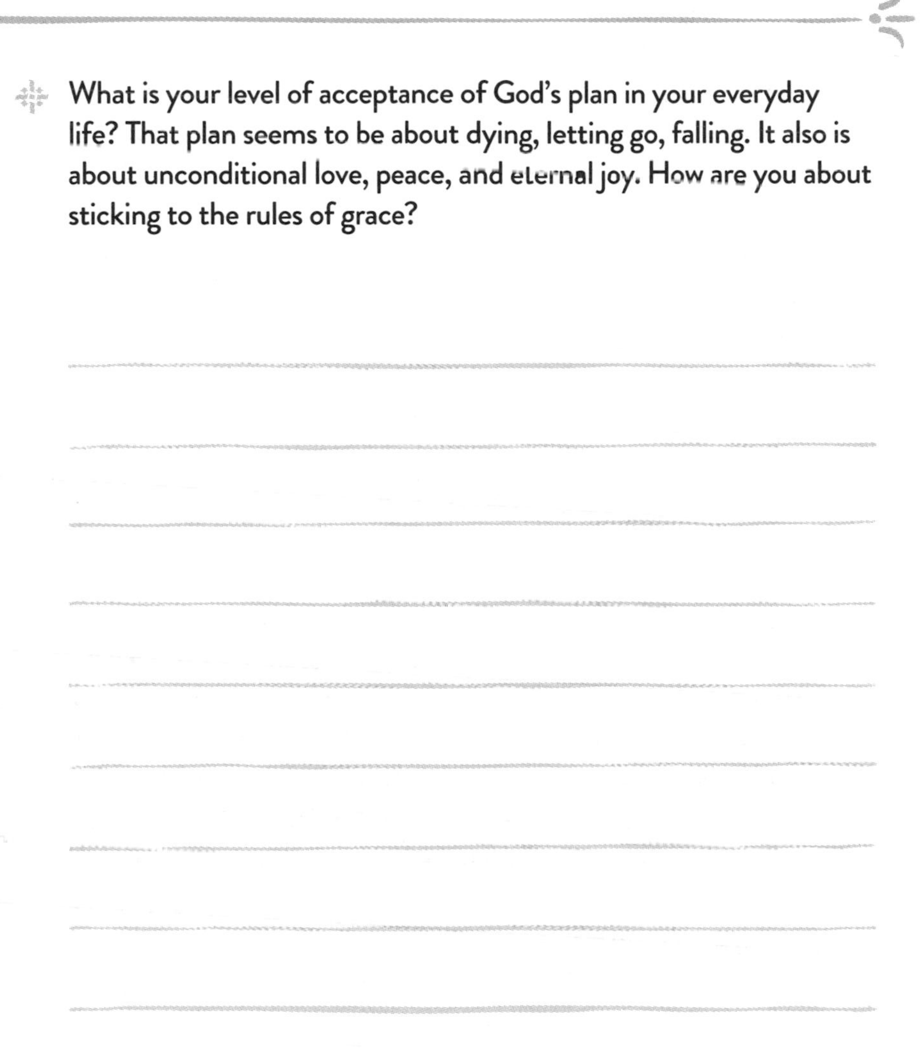

What is your level of acceptance of God's plan in your everyday life? That plan seems to be about dying, letting go, falling. It also is about unconditional love, peace, and eternal joy. How are you about sticking to the rules of grace?

Even in the small trials of life, it is hard to surrender...We want to handle situations, we want to make things happen....Think of life as a roller coaster. We ride the coaster, we don't drive it. **ELISABETH KÜBLER-ROSS**

We Experience Him Constantly

...He wills that we believe that we experience
Him constantly
(although we imagine that it is but little)
and by this belief He causes us evermore to gain grace,
because He wishes to be seen
and He wishes to be sought,
He wishes to be awaited
And He wishes to be trusted.

The alarm is an unwelcome intrusion into my dreams, and I stumble stiffly, groggily, to the bathroom. My day begins. Where is God? He is right here loving me, gently bringing me to consciousness, offering me a new day. As I age, that realization alone is precious. I have another day in which to experience my one paradoxical life of suffering and blessing. I must receive it with an open heart, no matter what this gift-package of a day may hold. The simple components of my morning routine offer blessing and call up gratitude. I lay out the vitamins, prepare our lunch salads, put away the air-dried dishes, and crack the egg for my husband's omelet, slurp-slurping it with a fork to break up the yolk. Here is the realization of love grown deep by constancy in small things. Here too is God, because all human love is divine love made manifest. I am grateful for forty-four years of the imperfect yet steadfast human loving of our marriage. Our partnership would dissolve without God's grace.

With breakfast laid out, I go carefully down the steps to the basement, still not fully awake. I slip my yoga tape into the player, by rote press the appropriate controls, and gingerly lower my still creaky self to my mat. As Rodney Yee begins our morning video routine, I carefully stretch into wakefulness. I am grateful for "Brother Ass" as Francis of Assisi calls the body, who has carried me through all my years. I can move and breathe, and I sense God in all my being. And so begins my day in which I believe I experience God constantly, although I know I am not constant in my awareness. His grace fills the gaps.

I turn over my little omelet in the frying pan
for the love of God. When it is done,
if I have nothing to do, I bow down
to the ground and adore God from whom has
come the grace to make it. **BROTHER LAWRENCE**

How are you aware of God's presence in your everyday life? Do you believe he is there even when you are not aware of him? For one moment, tap into God's deep, steadfast longing for you.

Seeking and Beholding

This vision was a teaching for my understanding
that the constant seeking of the soul pleases God very much;
for the soul can do no more than seek, suffer, and trust....

The seeking with faith, hope, and love pleases our Lord,
and the finding pleases the soul and fills it full of joy.
And thus was I taught for my own understanding
that seeking is as good as beholding during the time
that He wishes to permit the soul to be in labor....

A soul that simply makes itself fast to God with true trust—
either by seeking or in beholding—
that is the most honor that it can do to Him, as I see it.

Reading and rereading this passage, I keep coming to the same conclusion: God gives us points for effort! It is our effort of seeking him that pleases God. Sometimes we have a "for sure" experience of knowing his presence, his grace, his love that fills our soul and pleases us like nothing else on earth ever can. This, Julian says, is the *beholding*. We're in right relationship, and a little bit of the kingdom happens even now. But most of the time, it still feels like an awful lot of work! We are so distracted, so earthbound, so blind, really. As Julian advises, we must make ourselves *fast to God with true trust*. My morning prayer declares that all is for him! Then I get into the actual stuff of the day: the phone calls, the meetings, the torture of too soon deadlines, the cooking, the cleaning up, the trying to give my family fresh attention when I am dry as a corn husk blowing in a harsh wind. My everything cries out to seek *me*: my comfort, my opinion, my interests and desires, my way. I must say my morning prayer all day long until it loops right back into my evening prayer: "Take all my imperfect seeking, Lord. Though I got confused along the day, it really was all for you!"

Hearken to my words,
O LORD, attend to my sighing.
Heed my call for help, my king and
my God! To you I pray, O LORD; at dawn
you hear my voice; at dawn I bring
my plea expectantly before you. PSALM 5:1–3

Do you think of your life's purpose as seeking God? When do you know that you've found him? How has the seeking and beholding gone for you so far this day?

Three Objects in Our Seeking

It is God's will that we have three objects in our seeking:

*The **first** is that we seek willingly and diligently,*
without laziness, as much as possible through
His grace, gladly and merrily without
unreasonable sadness and useless sorrow.

*The **second** is that we await Him steadfastly because of His love,*
without grumbling or struggling
against Him, until our life's end (for it shall last only awhile).

*The **third** is that we trust in Him mightily in fully-certain faith,*
for it is His will that we know that
He shall appear without warning and full of
blessing to all His lovers—
for His working is secret,
but He wishes to be perceived,
and His appearing shall be truly without
warning.

Seek willingly; await steadfastly; trust in him mightily. Thank you, Dame Julian, for these instructions for my day! Now to live them out. When do I go from willingly to unwillingly? When there's just too much on my list, the deadlines are too tight, or I've seen too many people with problems, day after day. Something in me wants to push back. It doesn't take much for me to succumb to laziness. Give me a juicy novel, a bowl of any flavor of ice cream involving chocolate, and I can get very lazy and self-indulgent. When do I grumble or struggle? When things don't go *my* way: when the work I planned to accomplish gets lost in the midst of phone calls requesting help with other people's problems, things they could have solved themselves, things they could have done weeks ago, if they were organized. I do help, but grudgingly, while murmuring, grumbling, and inflating my own suffering. Then when the work is all done, I ruminate on how unjust all these requests were, how somebody's failure to plan is suddenly plopped at my doorstep and I am expected to save the day. I feel "put upon," and I lick my wounds while creating useless sorrow for myself and for my husband, who patiently listens to my complaints. God's ways are not my ways! Instead, when my plans get derailed, could I trust in his plans and flow with the new agenda, which situates me right where I am supposed to be, fulfilling the assignment God has given, rather than the one waiting on my to-do list? When I trust, he blesses and redeems the day with Plan B, which was really Plan A in his divine plan.

Examine your willingness, steadfastness, and trustfulness in regard to God's plan for your life. How much laziness, grumbling, struggling, and unreasonable sadness and useless sorrow creep into your daily round?

a LOT!

I Am God

See, I am God.
See, I am in everything.
See, I do everything.
See, I never lift my hands from my works,
nor ever shall, without end.
See, I lead everything to the end I ordained for it
from without beginning
by the same Power, Wisdom, and Love with
which I made it.
How would anything be amiss?

I wonder how my day would be different if I accepted and lived by these words of God to Julian. What if I worked at being very aware of God's hands on my day, of God leading everything to its proper end? I wonder if I would be less harried, less tired from the strain of trying to shape the day according to *my* will. Yesterday after visiting my grandsons, seeing people for spiritual direction, tending to things in my office, tidying up the house, figuring out the food, stopping at the library, I suddenly went AWOL. I took one of the new library books and a fistful of Halloween candy and shut the door of the sunny blue bedroom where I go to hide from all my responsibilities. The book soon swept me up in its plot and humor, and instead of the fifteen minutes I had consented to give it, two hours flew by. Feeling guilty that several things on my to-do list still remained, I emerged from my sanctuary determined to make up for lost time before supper. Mad at myself, growling inwardly, I resentfully tended to the rest of my work, knowing I had missed an opportune afternoon for planting the tulip bulbs, there being not many days left to complete this fall task. I had hoped to accomplish a significant chunk on a project in my office; well, now I was behind. By the time my husband arrived home, I was in a sour mood, too complicated to explain, so I sat at dinner in sullen silence. Poor guy thought he was at fault!

Rewind. What would this day have been if I had given it up to God instead of to my list? Would I have been more present to people, more intentional in my homemaking, more flexible in the ordering of tasks? Would my self-indulgence have been a gift of respite, God chuckling along with me at the humorous parts of the novel? Could I trust that God would give me another perfect afternoon to plant the hope of spring? Would I flow more gracefully with my day, knowing God was working his plan perfectly? Ahh. Nothing would be amiss.

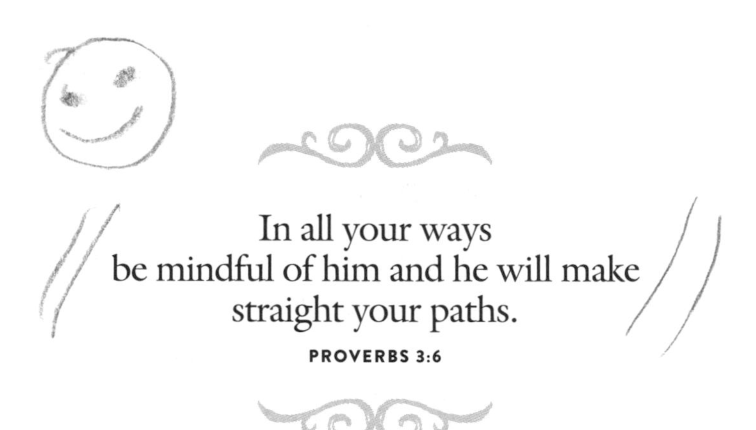

In all your ways
be mindful of him and he will make
straight your paths.

PROVERBS 3:6

Who plans your day, you or God? How do you react when your plans get derailed? Be aware, just for today, of God holding your day.

Joy and Sorrow

[God] showed a most excellent spiritual pleasure in my soul:
I was completely filled with everlasting certainty,
powerfully sustained without any painful fear.
This feeling was so joyful and so spiritual that I
was wholly in peace and in repose and there was
nothing on earth that would have grieved me.

This lasted only a while, and I was changed
and left to myself in such sadness and weariness of my life,
and annoyance with myself that scarcely
was I able to have patience to live.
There was no comfort nor any ease for me
except faith, hope, and love,
and these I held in truth (but very little in feeling).

And immediately after this, our Blessed Lord gave me
again the comfort and the rest in my soul,
in delight and in security so blissful and so powerful
that no fear, no sorrow, no bodily pain that could be suffered
would have distressed me.

And then the pain showed again to my feeling,
and then the joy and the delight,
and now the one,
and now the other,...

Julian accurately describes the divine game of "hide and seek" that I experience in my own life: sometimes the joy, and other times the sorrow. After sixty-four years I have gained a modicum of wisdom in realizing that neither state lasts, but one follows the other, over and over and over. It seems to be the rhythm of our time here in "earth school." I feel so "full up" when I watch my little grandsons. I recall my own labor-intensive days as a young mother and want to give my son and daughter-in-law little respites whenever I can. It is good to help out and to be a part of their circle of love. When I get back home and the late afternoon draws the curtains on the wet, fall day, I feel an emptiness as I miss my grown children, now all living their own fullness of life. There is a hollowness in my chest, and though I know God is here loving me in these lonely moments, I can't feel his love, and I wonder where it went so suddenly.

When does the divine/human game of "hide and seek" occur in your life? Are you able to keep faith during the times God seems to be hiding?

Pain Is Passing

But freely our Lord gives when He wishes,
and permits us to be in woe sometimes.

And both are one love,
for it is God's will that we keep us in this comfort
for all our might,
because bliss is lasting without end,
and pain is passing and shall be brought to
nothing for those who shall be saved.

And therefore it is not God's will
that we submit to the feeling of pains,
in sorrow and mourning
because of them,
but quickly pass over them and keep ourselves in
the endless delight which is God.

There is so much pain in the world, in our neighborhoods, in our families! As a mother the most paralyzing pain is when my children suffer. Then, for me, all is woe! Currently our family is grieving my son's divorce. I prayed fervently, every kind of prayer I know, for him and his wife to uncover one little spark among the ashes of a marriage neither had tended. In the busyness and crush of life, they had allowed the fire of their love to die. We needed a miracle here, but none was forthcoming. Is it God's will, then, that they part and begin anew, separately? This pierces my heart, this breaking of promises, this dying. Yet Julian says both the joy and the sorrow *are one love*. Simultaneous to all this pain, autumn flared its beauty, people were compassionate, and other healings were taking place in our lives. How to be grateful for the blessings, and not muck around in the woe?

I cannot ignore the pain, but can I experience it, do my grieving, without undue suffering, and still believe that the light is greater than the darkness?

When a woman is in labor, she is in anguish because her hour has arrived; but when she has given birth to a child, she no longer remembers the pain because of her joy that a child has been born into the world.

JOHN 16:21

When you or your loved ones suffer, how do you experience that pain without being completely overwhelmed by it? In these times is it still possible for you to believe in "the endless delight that is God"?

See How We Love Each Other

Because of the exalted, wondrous, special love
that He has for this sweet Maiden,
His Blessed Mother, our Lady Saint Mary,
He showed her highly rejoicing
(as in view of the intention of these sweet words)
as if He said:
"Dost thou wish to see how I love her,
that thou canst rejoice with me in the love that I
have in her and she in me? ..."

And so He wishes that it be known that
all those that delight in Him should delight in her
and in the delight that He has in her and she in Him.

The Lord grants Julian a vision of the wondrous love Christ has for his mother and she for him. In this moment of revelation, Julian glimpses their exalted love and sees that Jesus desires for us to share in it. So our Lord gives us sweet Mary as our own mother.

How do we share our love relationships with each other? Should each experience of true love and kindness be for all of us? I see an elderly gentleman take his wife's arm as they gingerly cross the icy parking lot to the grocery store. In the pew in front of me at church I see a young mother nuzzle the apricot down of her tiny babe's head. Looking out my front window, I see a teenage boy, growing from awkward to manly, saunter down my street to greet his fresh-faced bud of a girlfriend, hot sparks of attraction drawing them in. I learn tenderness, nurturing, and attraction by observing love in my neighborhood. Do my acts of love and kindness also beg to be shared? Might I be gracing the world with them, without even knowing it?

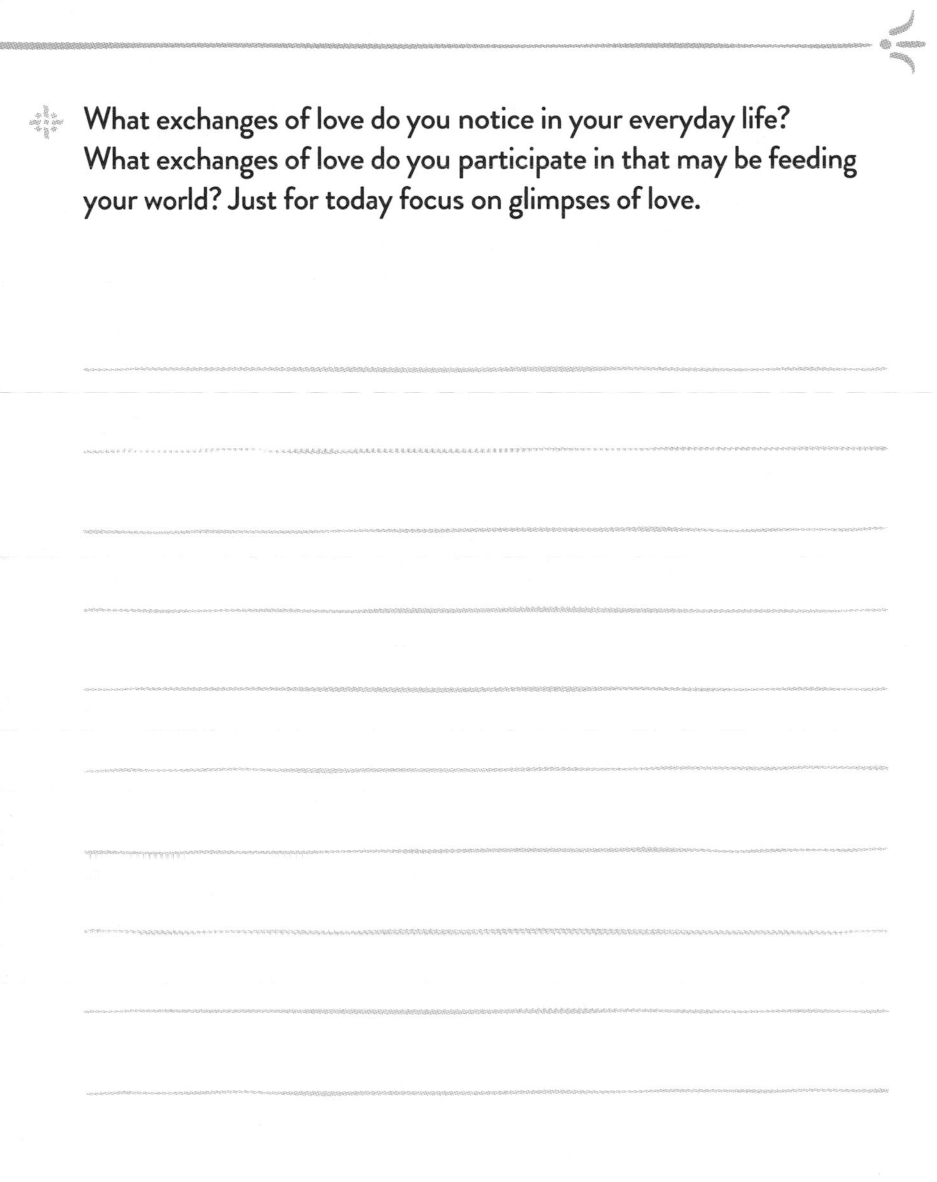

What exchanges of love do you notice in your everyday life? What exchanges of love do you participate in that may be feeding your world? Just for today focus on glimpses of love.

And this is my prayer: that your love may increase ever more and more in knowledge and every kind of perception… PHILIPPIANS 1:9

Why Sin?

After that the Lord brought to my mind
the yearning that I had for Him in the past,
and I saw that nothing stood in my way except sin
(and thus I observed universally in us all).
And it seemed to me that if sin had not been,
we would all have been pure and like to our Lord as
He made us,

And thus, in my folly, before this time I often wondered why,
by the great foreseeing wisdom of God,
the beginning of sin was not prevented,
for then, it seemed to me, all would have been well....

But Jesus...answered
by this word and said:
"Sin is inevitable,
but all shall be well,
and all shall be well,
and all manner of thing shall be well."

Sin is all around us, my own and that of others. I am appalled by the huge sins of the world—misuse of power, mass shootings, terrorism—but I am also disgusted by neighborhood sins of gossip, vandalism, and aggressive driving. When I see the newly finished bridge on Chase Avenue defaced with gang signs, when I must be careful not to step on broken beer bottles on my evening walk, and when I hear of the parishioner who has been embezzling from the festival funds, I shake my head in disbelief and am ashamed collectively for humanity. My current personal sin list: crabbiness

with my husband, judgment of colleagues, sloth. Like Julian, I wish sin never would have gotten a foothold in human history. As she was shown, sin is a barrier between us and God, and yet Jesus assures her that *all shall be well.* A paradox, yet a consoling one! In spite of our sin, God will make everything well!

Pray on the big sins, and the neighborhood sins, and ask to be made aware of your personal sins. Are you consoled by Jesus' assurance to Julian that "All shall be well"?

Jesus' Compassion

Thus I saw how Christ has compassion for us
because of sin....

For He says:
"I shall totally shatter you because of your vain
affections and your vicious pride;
and after that I shall gather you together
and make you humble and gentle, pure and holy,
by one-ing you to myself."

What is true compassion? It is different than pity, sympathy, or even empathy. *Com* (with)-*passion* is the willingness to enter into another's suffering and to walk the painful journey with that individual. Jesus has compassion for us in our sinfulness, even though he is witness to the great harm resulting from our sin. Julian is shown that sin serves a greater purpose in that it brings us to a state of helplessness that turns us malleable, makes us naked, and teaches us humility. Sooner or later we all must face our own compulsion to sin. My sin is uniquely mine, springing from my personality, my life circumstances, and my choices. It confronts me every day, begging for transformation. Too much of the time I ignore it and trudge down the same rut paths of ego and selfishness. Only now in my sixties is it becoming clear to me that I can choose a different path. I can be kind instead of critical; I can be grateful for what I do have; instead of "poor-me-ing" myself, I can choose joy in all the nooks and crannies of my daily round.

Be honest and list your sins. Pray now to feel the true compassion Christ has for you in your sinfulness. What "different path" must you choose to be free of the compulsion of your sin?

The Glorious Reparation

"Ah! Good Lord, how can all be well
considering the great damage that has come
by sin to Thy creatures?"...

To this our blessed Lord answered most gently,
and with most loving expression,
and showed that Adam's sin was the most harm that
ever was done, or ever shall be done, until the world's end....
Furthermore, He taught that I should observe the
glorious reparation,
for making this reparation is more pleasing
to the blessed Godhead and more valuable
for man's salvation, without comparison,
than ever was the sin of Adam harmful....

"For since I had made well the worst harm,
then it is my will that thou knowest from that
that I shall make well everything that is less bad."

God forgives the big sins and the small sins, all the sins. Can I do the same in my life? Can I forgive myself my own sins? When someone hurts me or is unkind to me or my loved ones, it wounds me deeply. I am more of a "feeler" than a "thinker," and so I walk around with my heart exposed most of the time. Adam and Eve's disobedience and all the sins of humankind that followed in the wake of that first sin must have hurt God profoundly—God,

who loves us like a "Papa." It seems to me that forgiveness is a process that I must always be working on. Unlike God, who forgave all our sins in one great act of salvific love, it takes me a while to forgive. I know that forgiveness must originate in my own heart. It doesn't really have to do with the act itself or even with whether or not the other person acknowledges his or her wrongdoing. Forgiveness has to do with my decision to no longer hold onto the hurt and resentment that consume me. Am I willing to see my offender as a child of God, imperfect and vulnerable to mistakes, just like me? In some instances it takes a lot of prayer to get to that place of my hard heart becoming "fleshy" again. I must courageously begin the process of forgiveness and draw on God's divine mercy to effect this transformation in my wounded self. It takes time.

The important
part of forgiveness
is to begin and to continue.
The finishing of it all
is a life work.

CLARISSA PINKOLA ESTES

What needs forgiving in your life? Are there wounds from the past that are still festering? Must you forgive a parent, a spouse, an adult child? Must you forgive yourself? Pray to be able to begin the process of forgiveness, and rely on the Holy Spirit to supply the courage you don't presently feel.

Rejoicing in Him

Our Lord wishes us to be engaged, rejoicing
in Him because He rejoices in us, and
the more abundantly we accept this with
reverence and humility,
the more favor we earn from Him and
the more help for ourselves;
and thus, we can see and rejoice that our
portion is our Lord,...
we should trust and rejoice
only in our blessed Savior Jesus, for everything.

Rejoice: to feel joyful; to be glad. Tigger of Winnie-the-Pooh fame comes to mind. Full of gladness, he engages in life, springing from one adventure to the next. Rejoicing in the sheer fact of his existence, he is bouncy and eager. But I wonder if true joy is something more than exuberance, and it is certainly more than fleeting happiness. As Julian uses the term "rejoice," it seems to refer to a fundamental orientation to life based in the knowledge that we are loved by God, who rejoices in us. And, she seems to suggest, if we could get this right, we would be more virtuous and at ease in our lives. It requires trust in the Lord. Can I for one day trust that God loves and delights in me? Being so cherished, can I go about my daily round rejoicing, perhaps with a little bounce in my step and a spring in my spirit?

How do you define joy? In what way is it different from happiness? What has been evidence of your rejoicing in the Lord today?

Joy does not simply happen to us.
We have to choose joy and keep choosing it every day.
It is a choice based on the knowledge that we belong
to God and have found in God our refuge
and our safety... HENRI NOUWEN

I Shall

And so our good Lord replied to all the questions and doubts
that I could raise,
saying most reassuringly:
"I am able to make everything well, and
I know how to make everything well, and
I wish to make everything well, and
I shall make everything well; and
thou shalt see for thyself that all manner of
thing shall be well."

When I repeat these lines again and again they give me comfort. Each day has its concerns of what might go well and what might go awry. Will I get everything done on my list, will my daughter get moving and sign up for health insurance, will my divorced son's heart heal so that he will be able to love again? Will the work I do for the church make an actual difference in someone's life? Will my little grandsons grow up to be healthy and happy? Will those who mourn be comforted? Will this? Will that? Julian had her questions and doubts, and so do I; so does each of us. I believe that God is able to make everything well. After all, God set this whole universe in motion and created every minute part of it. But what comforts me most in Julian's passage are the words *I wish to make everything well....* In those words I feel the love of God for his creatures, for me, and for my loved ones. We are so tiny and insignificant to the whole and yet God wishes to make all things well for us. Each time I ponder these words I am given an infinitesimal portion of "hazelnut grace" to believe that God cares tenderly for me and mine and for what we are about today. In some way, beyond my limited understanding, everything is going to turn out according to his plan. With this reassurance I can walk steadfastly into this day.

What are your questions and doubts? How does this passage speak to you and your concerns?

The Least Little Thing

...He wishes us to be aware that
not only does He take heed to noble and to great things,
but also to little and small things, to lowly and simple things,
both to one and to the other;
and so means He in that He says
"All manner of thing shall be well";
for He wills that we be aware that the least
little thing shall not be forgotten.

Some people reserve prayer for the big things: marital struggles, illness, loss of job, world peace. Yet Julian tells us that God concerns himself with *the least little thing*. I love this about God! Who else is so concerned about my little things? And so I pray to find a close parking spot in the congested area around the university, and to have the patience to listen to my brother's critical, ongoing lecture without getting angry and without judging him right back. I pray for rain for my dry garden, for clear roads in the winter, and for safe travel for my kids flying across the country. I pray for stamina to get back down in my office after lunch when the "slumpies" overtake me and I feel as though I am trying to move about in thick sludge. We share funny moments, God and I: insights, and epiphanies where at last I tell him, "Okay, I get it now." God is intimate with me, taking heed of all the comings and goings of my mind and heart. And though I repeat some of the same prayers every day, and I struggle with the same sins and compulsions, sometimes for years, he never gets tired of my least little things.

Do you go to God with the great things and the lowly, simple things? How do you know that he is listening? How might you open yourself to greater intimacy with him?

O Lord, you have probed me and you know me;
you know when I sit and when I stand;
you understand my thoughts from afar.

PSALM 139:1–2

Thou Shalt See for Thyself

Another understanding is this:
that, from our point of view, there are many deeds evilly done and such great harm given that it seems to us that it would be impossible that ever it should come to a good end;
and we look upon this,
sorrowing and mourning because of it,
so that we cannot take our ease in the joyful beholding of God as we would like to do;
and the cause is this:
that the use of our reason is now so blind, so lowly,
and so stupid that we
cannot know
the exalted, wondrous Wisdom,
the Power, and the Goodness of the blessed Trinity;
and this is what He means when he says,
"Thou shalt see for thyself that all manner of thing shall be well,"
as if He said,
"Pay attention to this now, faithfully and trustingly, and at the last end thou shalt see it in fullness of joy."

When my husband exclaims about something that he can't understand or thinks is unreasonable, such as why they build roundabouts to confuse the traffic at what used to be a perfectly good entrance ramp, or why there are extra charges on his utility bills (stuff he just doesn't get and thinks is stupid), I have taken to saying, "Well they must know something we don't." Who are "they"? The nebulous "someones" who are in charge of all the decisions we don't understand. A loving, merciful God is that "someone" who holds the blueprint of creation, and there's a lot that we don't understand, a lot that appears harmful, wasteful, and evil. Babies are aborted, typhoons destroy the homes of poor people, a vibrant young person takes her own life. How could "all be well"? Julian hears God saying that we must pay attention, have faith, and trust. All will work together and result in eternal joy! We must believe without presently being able to see or understand or even imagine how all will work together so that God's word comes to fruition.

So you also are now in anguish.
But I will see you again, and your hearts will rejoice, and no one will take your joy away from you. JOHN 16:22

In your life what remains a huge puzzle for you? What do you do with your longing to know and understand? In what instances must you practice faith and trust in God's eternal plan?

Rightfulness

Rightfulness is that thing which is so good
that it cannot be better than it is,
for God Himself is true rightfulness,
and all His works are done rightfully as they
are appointed from without beginning
by His high Power,
His high Wisdom,
His high Goodness.
And just as He ordained all for the best,
just so He works constantly and leads it to that same end;
and He is ever most pleased with Himself and with His works.
The beholding of this blissful agreement is most sweet to
the soul that sees by grace.

Right-full-ness. We might say, "Perfect!" or "Exactly!" or "Yes!" That thing which is so good that it cannot be better than it is! Or, we might say, "No!" or "Not now!" or "Not me!" or "Not this!" This is not rightfulness! Once when my Andrew was little, we had a crazy early May snowfall; heavy and wet, it snapped tree branches and caused tender yellow daffodils to cower in the ice. Andrew's usual morning practice was to come into our room while his Dad and I were still in bed and part the curtains on our bay window to see what the new day looked like. That morning he quickly withdrew his tousled blond head from behind the curtains and said in astonishment, "God made a mistake!"

Does God make mistakes? Julian says God is "true rightfulness" and all his works are planned from the beginning for the very best end, and he is constantly working his plan in all creation. Our choice is to cooperate with grace or to resist and suffer. I must remind myself daily to "get with the program." I can make my list, have plans and intentions, but I must always pray that my intentions for the day be aligned with God's intentions, and then adjust accordingly.

He is before all things,
and in him all things hold together.

COLOSSIANS 1:17

What is happening in your life right now that is contrary to what you think should be happening? Can you accept this thing as "rightful" according to God's plan, even though you cannot understand His purpose? How will acceptance change how you live in and through this experience?

Overly Low

Then He means thus: He wills that we be not carried overly low because of sorrows and temptations that befall us, for it has ever been this way before the coming of miracles.

Each human life will know pain. It is said that how much we suffer with our pain is up to us. Hmmm... I'm not sure what I think about that. But I do know that I can increase my pain by building a story around it, analyzing it, and trying to find its cause. How am I responsible for this pain? Has someone else contributed to it? Why would they possibly do that to me? What does this pain mean for my future? How will it restrict me and cloud over my joy? Poor me! My pain can take over, or I can choose to give it over. When I ask God to carry my pain, it is lighter. I put it at the foot of the cross because I know, in his infinite love, Jesus will suffer the pain for me. I set it aside beneath a celestial heating pad of golden grace light, which radiates over and through it. I bring light to someone else; then, in the beam of their joy, my pain begins to heal. I place my wounded heart in the Sacred Heart of Jesus, asking for transformation through the fire of his love. I do all these things while continuing to believe in miracles.

What do you do with your pain? Are your present sorrows overtaking your life? How might you give them over so as not to be carried overly low?

"I Keep Thee Full Safely"

Though our Lord showed me that I would sin,...
And in this I perceived a gentle anxiety,
and to this our Lord answered: "I keep thee full safely."

This word was said with more love and steadiness and
spiritual protection than I know how or am able to tell.
As it was shown that I would sin,
in just the same way was the comfort shown—

...And thus our Lord showed the completeness of love in
which we stand in His sight—
yea, that He loves us now as well while we are here
as He shall when we are there before His blessed face.

So because of the falling away from love on our part,
from ***that*** *is all our difficulty.*

Julian conveys God's love in such a way that I *feel* his sweet, tender love for me, though I am a sinner. Truly I am his little child, enfolded in his protection, kept always full safely. It makes me weep, the realization of it! The other day my little grandson Henry leaned too far on the door of the toy kitchen center and all the dishes and play food came suddenly crashing to the floor. His innocent little face immediately lost its happy countenance and was washed blank. Then his lower lip began to tremble and he backed away, wanting to flee the chaotic scene. "Oh, Henry, it's okay. It was an accident."

I scooped him up, his two-year-old self stiff with fear and remorse. Many hugs, kisses, and reassurances that Grandma wasn't angry with him were needed to restore his happy playing. O, Lord, I fall away from you, tripping over the tangles of my sinfulness. I long for you to scoop me up!

When do you experience the spiritual protection Julian describes in this passage? Do you believe God never stops loving you, even when you sin?

Sin Is the Harshest Scourge

Sin is the harshest scourge that any chosen soul
can be struck with.
This scourge chastises a man and woman terribly
and damages him in his own eyes to such an extent
that sometimes he thinks of himself as not worthy
except to sink into hell—
until contrition seizes him by the touching of the Holy Spirit
and changes the bitterness into hopes for God's mercy.
Then his wounds begin to heal...

Most preciously our good Lord protects us when it seems
to us that we are nearly forsaken and cast away
because of our sin and because we see that we have
deserved it.

And because of the humility that we gain in these troubles,
we are raised very high in God's sight, by His grace.

Julian tells us that God uses even our sin to our greater good. This is so hard for our small brains to fathom. When I sin (most recently the sin of judging another person, thinking I know what she should do with her life. Ha!), I feel terrible afterward. I know the thoughts I had or the words that came out of my mouth in that *know-it-all* tone were not really, truly me. They were a lesser, egotistic me, trying to grasp for some control over life, out of fear and insecurity and my own shame and woundedness. The aftermath of those judgmental thoughts and words is one of agitation, grasping, trying to convince myself of my "rightness." It is not love, or oneness, or peace. It is sinfulness, an awful state, a scourge. Yet, God is right there loving me, sending the Holy Spirit with hope for mercy, even though I am anything but deserving. I am humbled and healing begins...

Examine your most recent sin. Let yourself feel its scourge and how it turns you into someone other than your true self. Experience the kindly touch of the Holy Spirit on your battered soul, as healing begins...

Peace and Love

Our gracious Lord does not wish His servants to despair
because of frequent or grievous falling,
because our falling does not prevent Him from loving us.

Peace and love are always in us, existing and working—
but we are not always in peace and in love.

If only I could remember, when I am angry with my husband for driving so aggressively, that somewhere deep down inside of me are peace and love. When I work with someone who doesn't answer my phone calls, procrastinates, or keeps changing her mind about the project, I need to dig through the compost that covers my soul to find peace and love. Julian says they are always there, even if I am currently in free fall to sinfulness. When my daughter is traveling around the country to regions out of cell phone range, and I don't know where she is and I can't reach her, I must be content, knowing that getting back to peace and love is the best thing I can do. This will connect me with the peace and love that are deep inside her as well. Our gracious Lord is the source of all peace and love. When life pulls you out of your true self for whatever reason, breathe deeply and get back to the place of peace and love. It is within you.

As you live through this day, be aware of peace and love. When are you in? When are you out? What type of situations, people, and experiences tend to pull you out of peace and love? What works to get you back in?

Yearning

I understand truly that everything is prepared for us
by the great goodness of God
to such an extent that whenever we are ourselves
in peace and love,
we are truly safe.
But because we cannot have this in fullness while we are here,
therefore it is right for us evermore to believe in sweet prayer
and in love-filled yearning with our Lord Jesus.
He yearns ever to bring us to the fullness of joy...

All the time we are here on earth we will be *yearning* for the fullness of joy in God. We will experience moments of that fullness, get glimpses of it, and receive enticing hints of eternal bliss. But during this whole human life we are in the state of *yearning*. It is the "already but not yet" of which theologians speak. This makes the amassing of goods and the storing of stuff in barns (or rented storage units) ludicrous! This makes the seeking of titles, power, and country-club status much ado about nothing! Rather, Julian says, sweet prayer and loving are the pursuits of *yearning* for the fullness of life in God. In the everyday, can we take a "free-floating" stance of impermanence while living in a bricks and mortar world? Can we lean into the subtlety of always being "on the way," a "work in progress," "constantly becoming"? Every little prayer whispered in trust, and every kindness springing from true love, are the ways and means of *yearning* for what God has prepared for us.

In what areas of your life are you seeking definitive answers or desiring total control? What lies at the bottom of these desires? How might you let go a bit and float into yearning? How will you pray and love today?

Above all, trust in the slow work of God.

TEILHARD DE CHARDIN

Sure Trust

And yet frequently our trust is not complete,
for we are not certain that God hears us,
...because we feel absolutely nothing,
(for we are frequently as barren and dry after
our prayers as we were before).
...and He showed these words and said:
"I am the ground of thy praying—
first, it is my will that thou have something,
and next I make thee to want it,
and afterwards I cause thee to pray for it.
If thou prayest for it,
how, then could it be
that thou wouldst not get what thou askest for?"
...our good Lord shows a powerful encouragement,...

We pray and pray and pray and yet nothing moves; nothing changes. Or so it seems to us. Yet Julian explains that God places *desires* in our hearts so that we might ask for the fulfillment of those desires, so that in his bountiful love he can grant them. Why then does our praying leave us barren and dry? Julian explains it is our incomplete trust and uncertainty that cause the gap in this divinely designed circle of relationship. Perhaps we are too fixated on having the answers to our prayer come in exactly the "package" we had in mind. "No" is an answer; so is "wait." What seems to matter most, according to Julian, is that we continue to show up, voice our true desires, and trust God for the fulfillment. In all this, God encourages us powerfully! So pray on, even in emptiness and drought, longing for sweet relief. God hears and answers every prayer!

What prayers have you prayed for a long, long time, seemingly without fulfillment? What are the true desires of your heart in this instance? Might you be missing God's answer because you are awaiting your own answer? What helps you to persevere in prayer?

O God, you are my God whom I seek; for you my flesh pines and my soul thirsts like the earth, parched, lifeless and without water. PSALM 63:2

He Watches for Our Prayer

Most glad and happy is our Lord about our prayer,
and He watches for it
and He wishes to enjoy it,
because with His grace
it makes us like Himself in character
as we are in nature.

I'm a pretty low technology person, choosing to use my time differently (gardening, hiking, playing with the grandbabies). I'm not totally "Luddite"; I do text with my kids and a few close friends, and I have an email account I check every week or so at the library. Though I have a computer for my work, I've chosen not to have internet in my home office. My phone is not "smart," and I own nothing with an "i" in front of its name. These are all quality-of-life choices I've made, and I'm at peace with them. What strikes me in this passage from Julian is that God watches for our prayer and enjoys it when it comes. Yes, I know that feeling! Because I use electronic communication with only my family and close friends, I watch for their responses and enjoy them when they come! Though God knows every thought and feeling we have even before we articulate it, he still delights in communicating with us. This is how we keep our relationship close and growing, and the closer we get to him, the more like him we become. Prayer is the "love energy" between us.

Reflect on how you communicate with people. What is the quality of your communication? Is it hasty and reactive, or is it thoughtful and life-giving? And with God—what is the quality and frequency of your communication with God?

I love the LORD because he has heard my voice in supplication, because he has inclined his ear to me the day I called. PSALM 116:1–2

Pray Inwardly

He says this:
"Pray inwardly
even though it seems to give thee no pleasure,
for it is beneficial enough
though thou perceivest it not.
Pray inwardly,
though thou sensest nothing,
though thou seest nothing, yea
though thou thinkest thou canst achieve nothing,
for in dryness and barrenness,
in sickness and in feebleness,
then is thy prayer completely pleasing to me,
though it seems to give thee but little pleasure.
And thus all thy living is prayer in my eyes."

Every serious pray-er has at one time or another experienced periods when God appears to be busy elsewhere, and even the most heartfelt prayers seem not to get through. Or, our prayers lose their "juice"; we mumble words and light candles, in habitual, but empty motions. Prayer drought can last a long time, leaving us spiritually shriveled. The Lord instructs Julian that we are to persevere in the inward effort of prayer, though it gives us scant pleasure. Paradoxically, this barren and feeble prayer, in its poverty, is completely pleasing to God! It is not the felt sense of our prayer that matters, but that we continue to show up and express our longing for God, no matter our personal disposition at the time. Furthermore, the Lord says, this can be the orientation for all our living: an offering of ourselves to him. Thus, *all* becomes prayer.

Have you ever suffered dryness in your prayer? Did it last a long time and how did the drought end? Do you persevere in your prayer even when you don't get answers?

Cast your care upon the LORD,
and he will support you… PSALM 55:23

Prayer and Good Living

God accepts the good intention and the toil of His servants,
no matter how we feel,
wherefore it pleases Him that we work
both in our prayer
and in good living
by His help and His grace,
reasonably with good sense,
keeping our strength for Him
until we have Him whom we seek in fullness of joy,
that is, Jesus.

To work both in our prayer and in good living for God, seeking fullness of joy! What a noble desire, and yet we often go to our work with negativity, stress, and an impossible list of tasks before us. We work too long and too hard. The word "workaholic" has become a household term, and we race frantically to get more accomplished in smaller amounts of time. Today I must see people for spiritual direction, finish my plan for the class I will teach tonight, and send out handouts for a retreat I will preach in two weeks. Plus, I must tidy the house, run some errands, and figure out something more than a frozen pizza for supper. All the while, spring marches on and I have barely begun to tend my gardens. Everywhere I look in my house, clutter is multiplying and begging for order. I walk by without even a "lick and a promise" because I simply don't have enough time!

Julian also says we work *by his help*. Most days I'm trying to do it all myself, and not opening up to the very real help God wants to give me in my daily living. I can start by turning to him before beginning each task, opening to receive his help, seeking to know for sure if what I am about to undertake is even my assignment. Sometimes we load ourselves up with things that are not really ours to do. I can ask to be guided in my work by his Spirit, working for the highest good in cooperation and collaboration with others, and that I not get hooked into ego and control. I can seek to contribute the best of my gifts and then release my efforts, trusting God will use them to the best results in his plan, even if I never see those results.

God awaits us at every instant in all of our activities, in the work of each moment.

TEILHARD DE CHARDIN

What is your attitude toward your work? Do you seek God's help in doing it? What can you do to open yourself more fully to God's grace in your work?

Equally Great: Prayer and Trust

This is our Lord's will:
that our prayer
and our trust
be both equally great.

For if we do not trust as much as we pray,
we do incomplete honor to our Lord in our prayer,
and also we delay and pain ourselves;
and the reason is, as I believe,
because we do not truly acknowledge
that our Lord is the ground
on which our prayer grows,
and also that we do not recognize that prayer is given us
by the grace of His love.
For if we knew this, it would make us trust that
we would receive,
by our Lord's gift,
all that we desire.

I pray a lot. Do I trust *equally greatly*? If I'm honest, I would have to admit the doubt that creeps into my prayer quite frequently. I ask for the desires of my heart, and then I think about how those wonderful things are too much to ask for and how really bad things happen in the world and how I certainly don't deserve any of the things I'm asking for because I'm lazy and selfish. I remind myself that life isn't easy and challenges are there to make us grow. So, I reason, why would God consent to give me all these blessings, when what I really

Cast all your worries upon him
because he cares for you. **1 PETER 5:7**

need are more hardships to grow in holiness? After succumbing to all these doubts, my prayer is like a deflated balloon and I don't know why I'm even bothering to pray. Is this what Julian means by "delaying and paining ourselves"? The shoe seems to fit. What hurts worse is that this type of prayer "does incomplete honor to our Lord" because I am not fully trusting him and acknowledging him as the true ground of my being. I still want control; still want it *my* way.

What is the condition of your "trust muscle" in the present moment? Do you trust God as much as you pray or are you simply going through the motions, just in case? Do you honor God in your prayer by really believing that he hears and answers every prayer?

No Answer

But sometime it comes to our mind
that we have prayed a long time,
and yet, we believe
that we have not received our request.

However because of this we should not be sad,
for I am certain, in keeping with our Lord's purpose,
that either we are to await
a better time,
or more grace,
or a better gift.

I think we all, like St. Monica praying for the wayward Augustine, have prayers we have been praying repeatedly for the longest time, years even. We get tired of the prayers ourselves; does God tire of hearing them? "Hi, God, it's me, Jennifer. You already know what I'm going to say..." This "rut-praying" makes me sad, as Julian acknowledges. But she tells us not to be sad because God has something better in store for us. It will take more time, it requires more grace, and it is a far better gift than we can now imagine. Again, we must trust! Deep trust in God's plan for my life requires throwing myself over the cliff of trust. I have to let go completely. Meanwhile I pray on, trying to stay fresh, changing up my feeble prayers: same intentions, different devotions and prayer practices. I opt for creativity, just to be a little playful in the waiting and trusting. So today I pray the Rosary; this afternoon is silent meditation. I take the same desire of my heart to my *lectio divina*, and I offer my efforts of self-sacrifice in my daily round to purify my prayer. On Wednesday I lay all before the Blessed Sacrament at Adoration, and Sunday I am fed and consoled at Mass. Tomorrow I will have the opportunity to pray while walking an outdoor labyrinth. I pray; I wait; I trust. God loves and gives gifts. My prayer changes me and makes me ready to receive them gracefully, at the proper time.

What are your "rut prayers," those you've been praying for the longest time without seeming to get a clear answer? What are your devotions and prayer practices? Do you ever change them to keep your intentions fresh? How is your prayer changing you?

Understand and Pray

What He intends is this:
that we understand that He does everything,
and that we pray for that.
For the one is not enough,
for if we pray and do not ***understand*** *that He does it,*
it makes us sad and doubtful,
and that is not His honor.

and if we understand what He does, and we
do ***not*** *pray,*
we do not our duty.

And that way it cannot be,
that is to say, that is not the way He sees it,
but rather to understand that He does it ***and*** *to pray also,*
in that way is He honored and we are helped.

Julian explains that God is our foundation and he has everything that concerns us worked out to bring us to bliss. But we can't sit passively back and let the movie reel just roll. God calls us into relationship with him, and this relationship needs dialogue; it needs our prayer. The *understanding* and the *prayer* go hand in hand. One without the other is not what God intends for us. So, there must be no empty prayers: mumbled words done out of habit or "just in case." Rather our prayer must express our firm belief in God's plan for our lives, even when the details of the plan aren't all spelled out. And though we may not like what is happening presently, can we still accept that this too is part of God's plan and it is a plan for good? How much time and good energy are spent resisting what is! At times we lose our *understanding*; at other times we forget to *pray*. When these two come together, "*He is honored and we are helped.*"

Do you understand and pray? What do you think Julian is trying to express in this passage? How does it enlighten your own relationship with God?

For I know well the plans I have in mind for you,
says the LORD, plans for your welfare, not for woe!
Plans to give you a future full of hope. JEREMIAH 29:11

Prayer Ones the Soul to God

Prayer ones the soul to God;
for though the soul is ever like God in nature and essence
(restored by grace),
it is often unlike God in its external state
by sin on man's part.

Then is prayer a witness that the soul wills as God wills,
and it comforts the conscience
and inclines man to grace.

In this way He teaches us to pray and mightily
to trust that we shall have what we pray for,
for He looks upon us in love
and wishes to make us partners
in His good will and deed,
and therefore He moves us to pray for that
which it delights Him to do.

It is comforting to know that somewhere within this ego-encrusted, self-serving, mistake-prone, and downright confused self, there is a place where I am at one with God. And God created me thus, so I can never get too far off beam without being reminded to whom I belong. When I pray, I am closest to my true self and even my prayers have been seeded by God. My soul wants what God wants, no matter what my ego says. Now to get quiet and listen to my soul welling up within me, through the layers of my control freakishness, my unhealed and still smarting wounds, my utter humanness. Deep, deep within me are my true desires, and they are the very things God wants to give me. What do I desire more than anything? Only love!

Get still and really listen. Find that place where you and God are oned. What are the deepest desires of your soul? Do you believe God will satisfy these desires?

At the center point of our being is a point of nothingness which is untouched by sin and illusion, a point of pure truth, a point of spark which belongs entirely to God. THOMAS MERTON

It Surpasses All Our Imagining

Then I saw that His constant working in all manner of things
is done so well,
so wisely,
and so powerfully
that it surpasses all our imagining,
and all that we can suppose and comprehend.

And then we can do nothing more than to gaze at Him
and rejoice with a high mighty desire to be wholly
one-ed to Him,
and to pay attention to His prompting,
and rejoice in His loving,
and delight in His goodness.

When I ask God for things in prayer, I often have everything planned out as to the answer I want. Yet Julian is urging us to something higher when she shares her sight of God working constantly in all things to bring about results beyond our imagining. If we could see what she saw, we would gaze in awe and desire only what he has already worked out. That is true contentment: when my desires align with what God is already doing in a given situation. I read a quote once: "Happiness is loving what you have." It implies that what I have is truly what I need and that it is perfect in this moment. Can that be said for so-called "bad" things in my life, like illness or difficult relationships or childhood wounds or loud party-hearty neighbors? How can I love what I have in those moments? Can I trust that God is working in these things as well, and that these are things I need to experience in order for God's will to be ultimately brought to fruition in my life? This is a hard hazelnut, Julian, but I will ponder and pray on it.

Are you content with what you have? Can you truly love it and believe that God is constantly working in it to bring about fruits beyond your imagining? What aspects of your present life circumstances need a wider vision right now?

For this momentary
light affliction
is producing for us
an eternal weight of glory
beyond all comparison,
as we look not to what
is seen but to what is unseen;
for what is seen is transitory,
but **what is unseen
is eternal.**

2 CORINTHIANS 4:17–18

The Soul Does What It Was Made For

...continually the soul does what it was made for:
it perceives God,
it contemplates God,
and it loves God.

Because of this God rejoices in the creature
and the creature in God, endlessly marveling.

...he is created because of love
and in this love God endlessly keeps him.

The work of the soul goes on. I know that I am not always "tuned in" to God, and yet Julian describes this marvelous reciprocity between my soul and God that goes on endlessly, almost in spite of my will, my thoughts, my temptations, and my earthly desires. My heart beats; I take the next breath. I don't have to think about it. It is a natural rhythm, a flowing in and a flowing out. So too my soul, doing what it was made for: perceiving, contemplating, and loving God. Truly, we are wondrously made!

Stop for a moment. Come into the awareness of the work of your soul: perceiving, contemplating, and loving God.

As a deer longs for flowing streams,
so my soul longs for you, O God. PSALM 42:1

Self-Knowledge

And when we know and see truly and clearly what our self is, then shall we truly and clearly see and know our Lord God in fullness of joy.

How well do you know yourself? Your true self? Not the many selves you become to fill the roles in your life or the self you put on to please your boss or your spouse or your friends. In order to truly know myself, I must reflect on my words and actions and ask, "Where did that come from?" I have an "ego self" that gets me going in the morning and helps me face the world each day. It concerns itself with "making it" in life and has layers of expectation that permeate my reactions to life, like butter incorporated in the layers of puff pastry. Too cowardly to face the old hurts, fears, and jealousies, the detritus of my life, I hide much in the shadows. Sometimes though, on a day of unusual clarity I speak and act from the soul, a place of great love and peace, so true and perfect, I hardly recognize it comes from within me. Julian says when we truly know ourselves, we will know God.

How do you distinguish your true from your false self? On a daily basis are you reacting more from your ego self or responding more from your true self? Has this changed over the course of your lifetime? Do you long for a congruent life that is truly lived from the soul?

> Self-knowledge is so important that even if you were raised right up to the heavens, I should like you never to relax your cultivation of it...one day of humble self-knowledge is better than a thousand days of prayer.
>
> ST. TERESA OF AVILA

God's Mercy

But our good Lord, the Holy Spirit
(who is endless life dwelling in our soul)
full safely keeps us,
and makes a peace in the soul,
and brings it to rest by grace,
and makes it submissive,
and reconciles it to God.
And this is the mercy and the way in which our Lord
constantly leads us
as long as we are here in this changeable life.

Let us remember that this is a *changeable* life and that whatever is challenging now or is hurting now *will not* last forever. But whatever joy, love, truth, and beauty are present in our lives right now *will* last forever. Before my Mom died she told my sister that she hoped when she joined Daddy in heaven it would be like when they first met and fell in love. I pray that is true; I believe that is true. I believe the cutie boys' (my grandsons) smiles that light up my days will light up my heaven. I believe for all eternity I will be able to read and reread the Mother's Day card from my son that says, "You are the best, Mom!" I believe that my high school girlfriends with whom I laugh and cry will be there with me in heaven, laughing forever, and we will all be young again, eternally young. Julian tells us the Holy Spirit dwells in our souls keeping us even now in this endless life of peace and grace.

What will pass away, out of your changeable life, and what will remain for all eternity? Can you feel our Lord leading you to endless life today?

Whatever is true, whatever is honorable, whatever is just, whatever is pure, whatever is lovely, whatever is gracious, if there is any excellence and if there is anything worthy of praise, think about these things.... Then the God of peace will be with you. PHILIPPIANS 4:8–9

Mercy Works

Mercy works, protecting us,
and mercy works,
transforming everything into good for us.
Mercy, out of love, allows us to fail to a limited extent,
and in so far as we fail, in so much we fall;
and in so far as we fall, so much we die
for it is necessary that we die
in as much as we fall short of the sight and sense of God,
who is our life.

We pray: *Lord, have mercy. Christ, have mercy*. I often end the prayers I write in my journal: *Jesus, Mary, and Joseph, have mercy on us*. The psalms speak often of God's mercy. Julian says mercy is our safety net as we daily live the Paschal Mystery of Jesus, each unique cycle of suffering, death, and resurrection. Mercy works! If I could see my life in God's eyes I would see the countless times he has protected me, hanging on steadily as I edge away. He never gives up and loves me even when I am in the throes of jealously, revenge, and selfishness. If mercy were fluorescent, I would see it glow in my darkest moments, a beacon of hope. I do not always have eyes to see and so I miss realizing how God is unendingly merciful to me. The quotidian mercies blend into the landscape of my day, and so I forget to be grateful for hot water and creamy goat's milk soap, for the microwave cooking my oatmeal so very quickly, for the trucks that salt my road, for the good-bye kiss of my dear husband. Even the pneumonia I suffered through during the holidays now has me rejoicing that I'm not coughing my brains out every day. God loves me and is transforming everything into good for me!

Do you have eyes to see God's mercy in your everyday life? Can you fall into his safety net of love and care for you? Even in the dark times? Especially in the dark times?

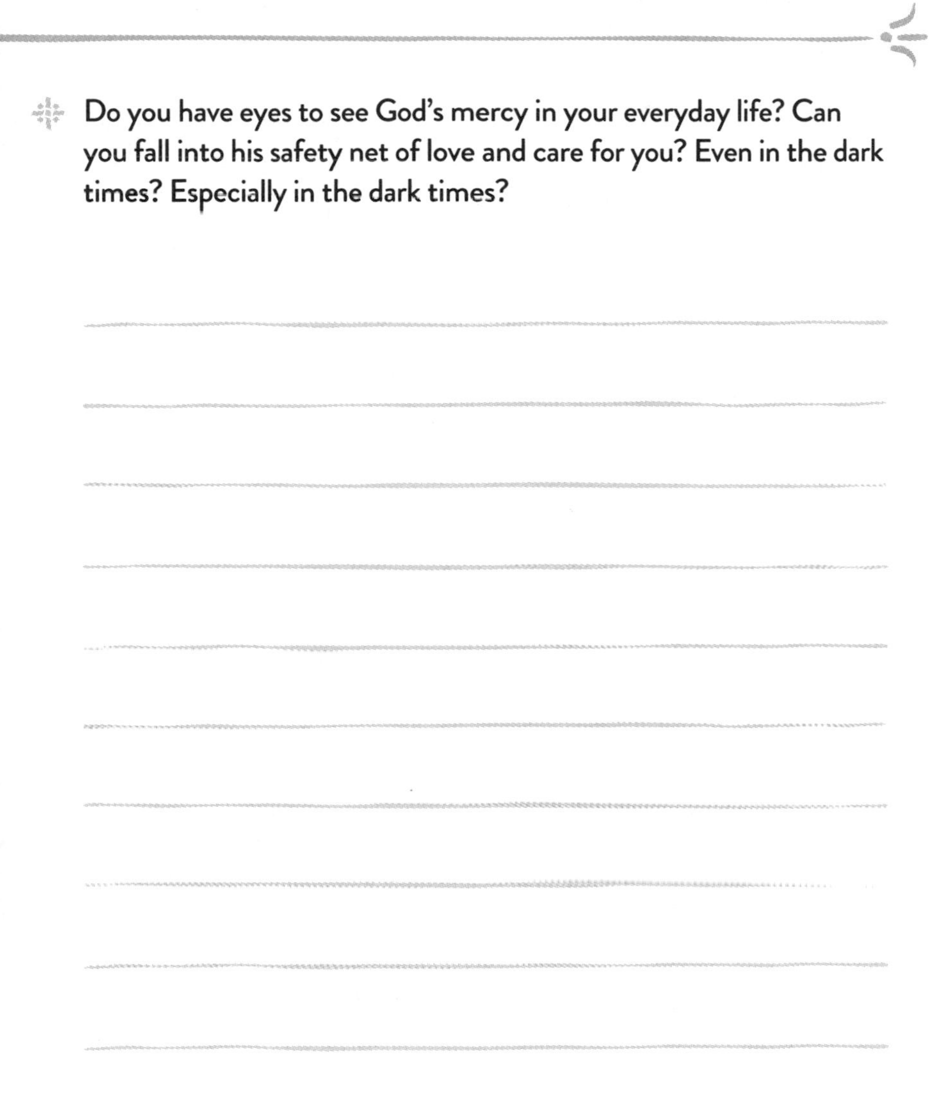

Slow me down, Lord. I am going too fast.
I can't see my brother when he is going past.
I miss a lot of good things, day by day.
I can't see a blessing when it comes my way.

AUTHOR UNKNOWN

Enwrapped in God

Although we feel miseries,
disputes
and strifes in ourselves,
yet are we all mercifully enwrapped
in the mildness of God
and in His humility,
in His kindliness
and in His gentleness.

"Enwrapped" is one of my favorite Julian words. To me, it speaks security and love. When I am distraught I hike into deep woods for the secure enclosure. My red flannel sheets open like a snug, padded envelope at the end of a damp, cold winter's day. When I am barely hanging on, the prayers of my friends and loved ones gently encase my miseries with heaven-spun gauze. The strong embrace of my husband's arms draws away the exhaustion of the day. The "monkey hugs" of my little grandsons, their small arms clinging around my neck, are elemental love. We humans need holding; God enwraps us.

When do you feel enwrapped in God's love? How do you hold and allow yourself to be held by others?

And yet I raise my hands aloft to God,
that I might be held by God, just like a feather
which has no weight from its own strength
and lets itself be carried by the wind.

ST. HILDEGARD OF BINGEN

Contrariness Made Sweet

And that contrariness which is now in us,
Our Lord God of His goodness makes most profitable for us,
because that contrariness is the cause of
our tribulations and all our woe,
and our Lord Jesus takes those
and sends them up to heaven,
and there are they made more sweet and delectable
than the heart can think or tongue can tell.
and when we come there, we shall find them ready.
all transformed into truly beautiful and
endless honors.

My little grandson Leo, cute as a button, is intensely caught in the contrariness of a two-and-a-half-year-old. In every task he asserts, "Do it myself!" and to every question he responds with the opposite of what would be most practical, easeful, and really, well, what the adults would like him to do. So if you offer him juice, he wants milk. When you pour his milk, he insists on "Juice!" Several times a day his contrariness so entangles him, he ends in a distraught puddle of protest and flailing limbs. Leo really is a sweet little boy. The "terrible twos" won't last forever.

After his nap (life is planned around Leo's nap!), he wakes, rosy-flushed and cherubic, his face alight with a happy grin, all transgressions forgiven and forgotten, ready to begin again. He is now so happily "re-booted" I think he must visit heaven in his dreams!

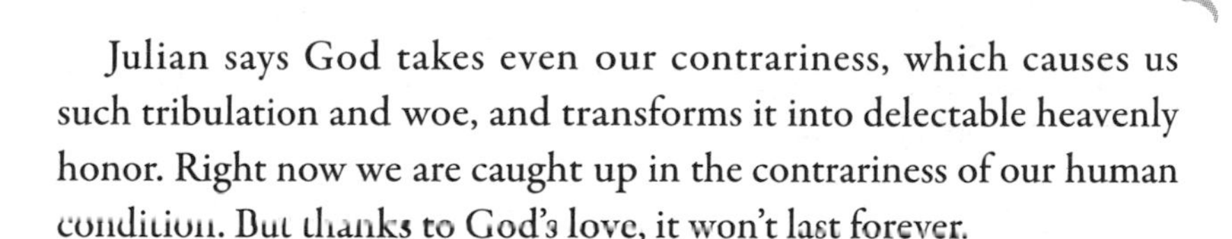

Julian says God takes even our contrariness, which causes us such tribulation and woe, and transforms it into delectable heavenly honor. Right now we are caught up in the contrariness of our human condition. But thanks to God's love, it won't last forever.

When do you feel most "contrary to your life"?

Steady by Grace

...at any time we fall by our blindness and our misery,
that we can readily arise,
knowing the sweet touching of grace,
and willingly amend ourselves
following the teaching of Holy Church according to the sin's gravity,
and go forthwith to God in love,
neither on the one hand fall overly low,
inclining to despair,
nor on the other hand be over reckless as if we gave no heed,
but humbly knowing our weakness,
aware that we cannot stand even a twinkling of an eye
except by the protection of grace,
and reverently cleaving to God, trusting in Him alone.

In our friendships, family relationships, and work and neighbor relationships, we frequently quarrel, hold grudges, and let one another down. We don't always treat people justly, nor do we love perfectly. Yet God in his grace lifts us up each time we fall. We get another chance; we are forgiven; the slate is wiped clean! This *sweet touching of grace* is given again and again in a human lifetime. Julian advises balance: don't incline to despair when you sin; but don't sin boldly as if nothing mattered. To be truly *humble* is to acknowledge our weak humanness while trusting in God's unconditional love and mercy.

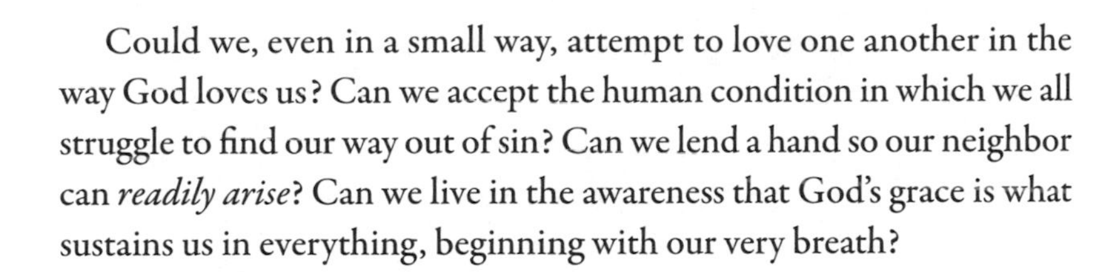

Could we, even in a small way, attempt to love one another in the way God loves us? Can we accept the human condition in which we all struggle to find our way out of sin? Can we lend a hand so our neighbor can *readily arise*? Can we live in the awareness that God's grace is what sustains us in everything, beginning with our very breath?

When in the course of your day are you aware of the "sweet touching of grace"? When you fall into sin are you open to Christ's redemption? How do you help others "readily arise" out of their sinfulness?

Double Action

There is absolutely nothing separating the one and the other,
for it is all one love.

This blessed love has now in us a double action:
for in the lower part are
pains and sufferings,
compassions and pities,
mercies and forgiveness
and such other things that are beneficial,
but in the higher part are none of these,
except the same high love and overwhelming joy,
in which overwhelming joy all pains
are wholly destroyed.

In this our good Lord showed not only our excusing,
but also the honorable nobility that He shall bring us to,
transforming all our guilt into endless honor.

Julian comes to understand there are two parts to our existence: our earthly life (the lower part) and our life of full union with God, yet to come (the higher part). There is no doubt that we all struggle here in this lower part, and that whatever we may attain in worldly goods, esteem, or accomplishment does not last. What lasts is love and joy! If only I could remember that truth when the pains and sufferings come, I could perhaps find their deeper benefit. If only I could embrace the need for compassion, mercy, and forgiveness, I could cooperate with the process of the "rock tumbler" of life, instead of resisting it.

Only if I can live this lower part well can I be transformed to receive the honor of the higher part.

Do you accept, even embrace, the pains and sufferings of this lower part? How do you experience the compassions, pities, mercies, and forgiveness inherent in your earthly life so as to reap their benefit?

...you will weep and mourn, while the world rejoices; you will grieve, but your grief will become joy...But I will see you again, and your hearts will rejoice, and no one will take your joy away from you. JOHN 16:20, 22B

Never Consent to Sin

In this showing I saw and understood full certainly
that in every soul that shall be saved is a divine will
that never consents to sin, nor ever will.

This will is so good that it can never will evil,
but evermore continually it wills good
and does good in the sight of God.

There is good in everyone and it is that good, according to Julian, that will never fully consent to sin. This is because we are made in the image and likeness of God and so there is divinity deep within us.

Archbishop Desmond Tutu once said to Franciscan Richard Rohr: "*We are only the light bulbs, Richard, and our job is just to remain screwed in.*" Jesus said not to keep our light under a bushel basket. So I must pray, do good works, forgive, love, and go daily to his word to receive my next instruction. I must live in the "illumined NOW" so as to shine out the light of Christ, to dispel the darkness.

On any given day, what aspect of yourself do you cultivate? Does your human tendency to sin get all the press, the energy, the time, the "juice" of your being? Or, do you strive to be like God: forgiving, loving, new, open, possible, large? Does your divine nature wither or grow?

Before Ever He Made Us, He Loved Us

Before ever He made us, He loved us,
and when we were created we loved Him.
And this is a love created
by the natural essential Goodness of the Holy Spirit,
mighty by reason of the Power of the Father,
and wise in reminder of the Wisdom of the Son,
and thus is man's soul made by God
and at the same moment knit to God.

The needs of the day tear at me by bits, and I feel so disjointed, trying to respond in multiple directions simultaneously. Work outlines the day, but people call and cancel or want to change their appointments according to their convenience. Of course, I accommodate them, but then my prayer time is edged out and I am missing my grandsons. The autumn day is lovely, and I want to sit and let the shocking red maple leaves snow down on my head. Oh, and what are we having for supper, because, being human, we do have to eat!

But then Julian reminds me of a love that knits me to God. A love that was *before ever*! Below the static of schedules, domestic duties, and the intrusive beeps of technology, even deeper down than all the needs of those I love, is my soul, made by God. No matter how scattered, disjointed, and flying apart I may feel in any moment, I am really more "together," more tightly, rightly, "knit," than I can even perceive. On a soul level, I couldn't be any more connected than I already am. Thank you, Blessed Trinity, for loving me into your tightly knit circle!

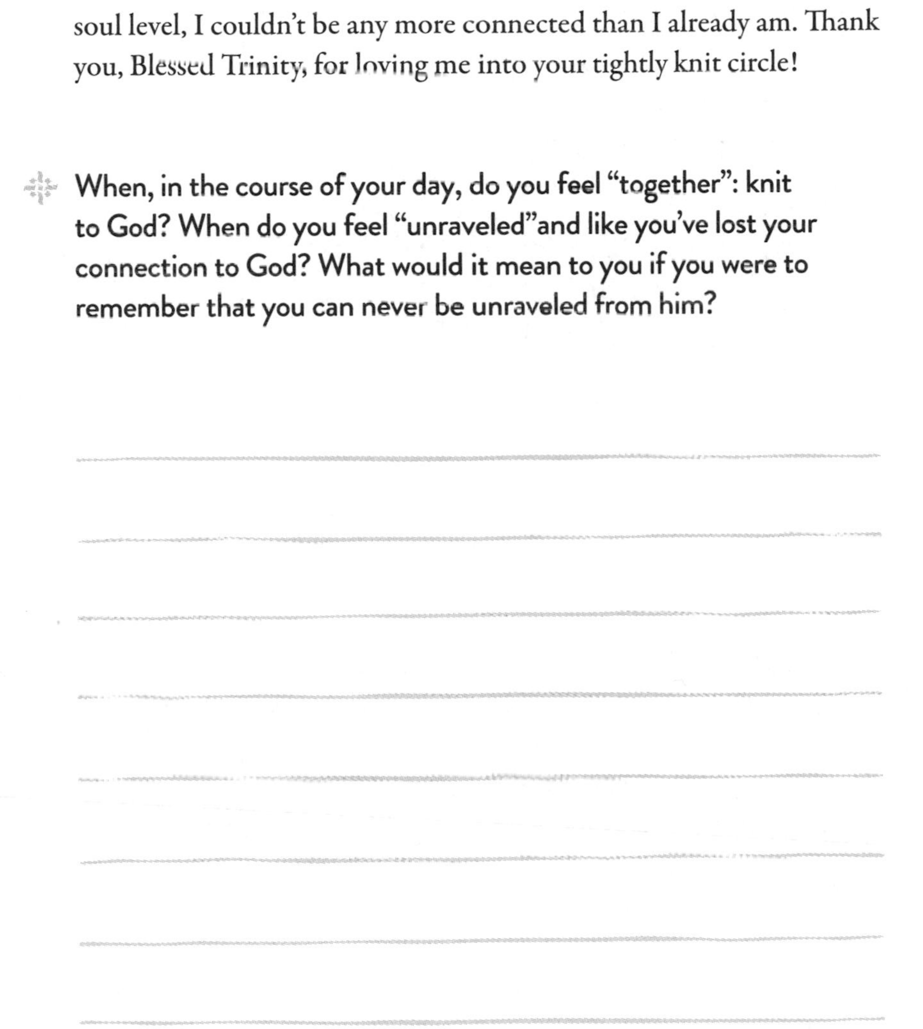

When, in the course of your day, do you feel "together": knit to God? When do you feel "unraveled"and like you've lost your connection to God? What would it mean to you if you were to remember that you can never be unraveled from him?

For just as the body lives from the soul, so does the soul live from God....It lives as one spirit with him. ST. WILLIAM OF ST. THIERRY (12TH CENTURY)

Enclosed in the Trinity

We are enclosed in the Father,
we are enclosed in the Son,
and we are enclosed in the Holy Spirit;
and the Father is enclosed in us,
and the Son is enclosed in us,
and the Holy Spirit is enclosed in us:
all Power,
all Wisdom,
all Goodness,
one God,
one Lord.

Newborn babies must be swaddled firmly and held closely in this world. After all, they grew into being in an enclosure perfectly designed to meet their needs: warmth, nutrition, the rhythmic swish of fluids, and the firm and loving heartbeat of their mother. When they are born into this world, they do not forget from whence they came and so they seek all the elements of their former world: warmth, nutrition, security, mother.

As we grow accustomed to our humanity, our secure origins begin to fade from our consciousness, yet in our truest, deepest self, we long for home. Julian reminds us that we have never lost that perfect place of beginning—that, in truth, we are even now swaddled in the power, wisdom, and goodness of the Trinity. Given this knowledge, we never have to feel lost, forsaken, or without hope, no matter how dire our earthly circumstances may appear.

Throughout your day, detach from all the "doings" and rest a moment in the perfect enclosure of Trinitarian love. All you need is right here.

Faith Is a Right Understanding

Faith is nothing else but a right understanding
(with true belief and certain trust)
of our being—
that we are in God,
and God in us—
which we do not see.

I love how Julian boils things down to their essence. Faith, which seems big, theological, and complicated most of the time, becomes clear, simple, and immensely profound in her explanation. Faith is an understanding of right relationship: God and me—one! I believe this; I trust this. I cannot see this with my earthly eyes, yet I have faith.

Faith means I step into the unknowns of this day, knowing I am loved and cherished. So as I do my morning yoga, I marvel at this body God has made. Just my toes alone are fascinating—how they all line up, stretch, and give me balance as I stand. God's design! In an hour I will go to care for three of my grandchildren: God's love manifested as human cherubs! Later as I companion people in spiritual direction, God is with us, shedding light, giving understanding, and nourishing souls. In the late afternoon the winter sky turns azure blue just at the horizon, soft grayness above and snowy luminosity below. Black tree silhouettes vein through the tripart swash of color and light. God's masterpiece! All day long I am in God, and God is in me: Faith!

Does Julian's explanation of faith resonate with you? What sense of unity do you experience with God throughout your day?

Coming Up to Our Essence

In this action the Holy Spirit forms in our faith the hope
that we shall come again up to our essence,
into the strength of Christ,
increased and fulfilled through the Holy Spirit.
Thus I understand that the fleshliness is based
in nature,
in mercy,
and in grace,
and this basis enables us to receive gifts
which lead us to endless life.

Hope is planted deep within the soil of our souls. The hope of "coming up" to our true selves, our Christ-selves, is hardwired into us. It is said that "hope springs eternal." Without God, with only our *fleshliness*, the trials of this life would soon cause us to despair. Where there is life, there is hope. This is God's design. Yet, I know it is tempting to give up, to fall into victim mode, and to say life is all too hard and too complicated and I just can't do it anymore. No, I can't. Not on my own. My husband and I have been replaying some of our marital struggles: some of those same "growing edges" that have plagued us for forty-three years. They come

Do not look forward to the
changes and chances of this life
in fear; rather look to them with full hope
that, as they arise, God, whose you are,
will deliver you out of them.

ST. FRANCIS DE SALES

from personality and gender differences, from different perspectives of what a marriage should be, from childhood wounds and fears. We are so weary of the repeated nature of the struggle: promises made, promises broken. We aren't doing this very well on our own. Yesterday, while looking through some old files, I came across a "Couple's Prayer." I made two copies and asked if we could pray this prayer together in the morning and the evening. He agreed. We asked God to bring us up higher into the strength of Christ, so our marriage could be increased and fulfilled through the Holy Spirit. It's never too late. *Where there's life, there's hope.*

In your life, where is hope? Where is the temptation to despair? Turn to the Lord today with hope and ask for the grace you need for the struggle of this fleshly journey.

The Holy Spirit Breathes into Us Gifts

All the gifts that God can give to creatures He has given
to His Son Jesus for us.
These gifts He, dwelling in us, has enclosed in Himself
until the time that we are grown and matured,
our soul with our body
and our body with our soul
(either of them taking help from the other),
until we are brought up in stature as nature works,
and then, on the basis of human nature
with the action of mercy,
the Holy Spirit graciously breathes into us
the gifts leading to endless life.

Every day is a gift, and every day is a lesson from the Holy Spirit. The giving of the gifts, as Julian describes it, takes time. Living takes time, and the soul and the body work together, helping each other. Since I reached the crossroads of age sixty (a birthday that felt more significant than any I can remember, maybe since eighteen!), both the lessons and the gifts have been coming in abundance. It has taken years for the Holy Spirit to pry me open, so tight in the ego bud was I encased! The gargoyles of old ruts and judgments are slowly dissolving. Setting down resistance that exhausts my strength, I am opening more willingly now to God's plan for my life. The Holy Spirit breathes into me and through me the very life of God! Each new day is holy and precious!

Are you opening more every day to receive the gifts of the Holy Spirit? Are your soul and your body working in mutuality? How so? How not? What "gargoyles" are slowly dissolving? To what resistance are you clinging?

God, the supreme artist, fashions and continually refashions his special creation, human beings, whom he never deserts.

ST. HILDEGARD OF BINGEN